Three Simple Questions

for Youth

KNOWING THE GOD OF LOVE, HOPE, AND PURPOSE

A Six-Week Study for Youth

ABINGDON PRESS
NASHVILLE

THREE SIMPLE QUESTIONS
LEADER GUIDE

Written by Amy Valdez Barker
Edited by Josh Tinley
Cover Design by Marcia C'deBaca

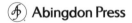 Abingdon Press

ISBN-13: 9781426742613

Manufactured in the United States of America

11 12 13 14 15 16 17 18 19 20— 10 9 8 7 6 5 4 3 2 1

CONTENTS

Three Simple Questions
Introduction

Human beings are curious. We like to ask questions. Moses, after receiving God's call from the burning bush, responded with a litany of questions: "Who am I to go to Pharaoh?" (Exodus 3:11); " 'What's this God's name?' What am I supposed to say?" (3:13); "What if they don't believe me or pay attention to me?" (4:1).

While Israel was being oppressed by Midianites, Gideon asked, "With all due respect, my Lord, if the LORD is with us, why has all this happened to us?" (Judges 6:13). David began Psalm 22 by asking, "My God! My God, why have you left me all alone?"

Asking questions is in our DNA. We are created in the image of a God who often uses questions to teach us and guide us. When Job complained to God about his suffering, God answered him with questions: "Where were you when I laid earth's foundations?" (Job 38:4); "Who is wise enough to count the clouds?" (38:37); "Will the one who disputes with the Almighty correct him?" (40:2). Jesus asked his disciples, "Who do people say that I am?" and then asked Peter, "Who do you say that I am?" (Mark 8:27, 29).

As Christians we have plenty of questions about God and our faith. We want answers about who we are and why we're here and what we're supposed to do. We want to know about God and God's will and what God has in store for us. There is no end to the questions we could ask.

This study, which is based on Rueben P. Job's book *Three Simple Questions: Knowing the God of Love, Hope, and Purpose*, looks at three questions regarding God and our faith: Who is God? Who am I? and Who are we together? Our answers to these three simple questions have big implications for how we answer all the other questions that arise. Our answers to these questions also say a great deal about how we live our lives as God's people and disciples of Christ.

Youth and the Three Simple Questions

Young people especially like to ask questions. They're reaching an age where they no longer take for granted the things that they learn from adults. They are no longer content with facts or statements; they want to know "why?" and "how?"

Those of us who work with youth need to assure them that their questions are not off-limits. It's OK for them to question things they've learned. And it's OK for them to want to know more and to ask, "Why?" or, "How?" We need to provide for them a safe space to ask and to wrestle with tough questions of life and faith. At the same time, we must teach youth where to go for answers. They need to know that they can look to Scripture, the person and example of Jesus Christ, and our ongoing experience of the Holy Spirit to better understand who God is, who we are, and who we are together.

Teaching Three Simple Questions

The goal of this study is to get youth to think critically about God, what it means to be a child of God, and what it means to be part of Christ's body, the church. While this study is based on three simple questions, youth should not come away from it with three simple answers. Instead, these questions should get them thinking about all aspects of their relationship with God and their identity as a follower of Christ.

The six sessions in this study are divided into three, two-session units: one unit for each of the three simple questions. The key teaching points in each session come from Rueben P. Job's book, *Three Simple Questions: Knowing the God of Love, Hope, and Purpose.*

Investigations and Optional Reading Assignments

All six sessions in *Three Simple Questions for Youth* conclude with an "Investigation" that asks them to look at ways that God is at work in their lives during the week between sessions. Five of the six Investigations include three clues based on what the youth learned in that week's session. The Investigation for the final session is a "30-Day Means of Grace Challenge" in which youth will commit for an entire month to daily practices of prayer, Scripture reading, and acts of mercy.

The first session in each unit includes an optional Reading Assignment that asks youth to read a chapter of *Three Simple Questions* in the coming week and to reflect on a few questions as they read. Groups who choose to do these assignments can, in the second session of each unit, debrief what they have read.

Who Is God?
Introduction

Our identity is found and formed by the God we worship and serve. Our life together as Christians is discovered, held together, and lived out based on our understanding of the God we have come to know and seek to follow.

—**Rueben Job,** *Three Simple Questions*

Throughout history humans have asked big questions such as, "Who are we?" and "Why are we here?" For many of us the answers to these questions involve God. But that brings up another question: "Who is God?"

As Christians we know that God created and loves each one of us and wants to be in relationship with us. We also know that God calls us to be in relationship with our fellow humans. These truths lead each of us back to the questions, "Who is God?" and "Who am I?" They also raise another question, "Who are we together?" For the next six weeks we'll take a close look at these three simple, yet complex, questions.

We'll begin by asking, "Who is God?" This simple question has a million answers. But as Christians, we see God most clearly through the persons of Jesus, who lived on the earth as one of us, and the Holy Spirit, who lives in us and among us. In the first two sessions, we'll look at Scripture and draw from our experiences and the experiences of others as we wrestle with this first question.

7

Youth and the Question

"Who is God?" is an age-old question that billions of people throughout history have asked and that people will continue to ask for years to come.

Maybe teens ask this question because they want to challenge simplistic descriptions of God that they heard as children or to rebel against what they have learned in Sunday school. Or maybe they truly want to know the answer to the question, "Who is God?"

The challenge for those of us who work with youth is to approach this question in a way that opens teens' minds to all the possibilities and responses that arise when they seek to understand God, without opening their minds so widely that they become lost in the unknown.

Will there ever be an answer to this question that can satisfy the inquisitive mind of a young soul? Perhaps not. But we must create an environment where youth can wrestle with this question and can draw on Scripture and church teaching as they seek an answer.

Teaching These Sessions

Question 1: Who Is God? Part 1

Session 1 introduces youth to the three simple questions, focusing specifically on the first question. The purpose of this session is for youth to reflect on a question that Christians often take for granted. "Who is God?" seems simple enough, but how we answer this question has an impact on what we believe, how we live, how we relate to God, and how we relate to other people.

Answering this question is not just an intellectual exercise. We answer the question through our words, actions, and relationships. When making money is our top priority, we name wealth as a god. When we care more about people liking us than being faithful to Christ, we name popularity as a god.

This session not only asks, "Who is God?" but also it challenges youth to think about the gods they name through the way they live.

Question 1: Who Is God? Part 2

"Who is God?" is a big question, but it's one that God answers. God came to live among us in the person of Jesus. In Jesus we see God's love, faith, compassion, and justice in the flesh. While Jesus no longer lives among us on earth, God continues to be present with us in the person of the Holy Spirit, who offers us comfort, guidance, and strength.

Session 2 explores how we know God through Jesus and the Holy Spirit. Youth will study Scriptures that describe these persons of the Trinity, how they relate to us, and how they relate to one another and God the Father.

As you teach this session, help youth to think critically about what they know about Jesus and what this knowledge says about God. Challenge them to identify ways that they have felt the presence of the Holy Spirit.

Basic Supplies for This Study

The following supplies will be used frequently throughout this study, so they will not be listed in the supplies for each activity:

- Bibles
- Student books
- Paper
- Pens or pencils
- Markerboard and/or large sheets of paper
- Broad-tip markers
- Copy of *Three Simple Questions,* by Rueben Job, for each youth (optional)

How we answer the
question, "Who is God?"
has an impact on what
we believe, how we live,
how we relate to God,
and how we relate to
other people.

Question 1: Who Is God?
Part 1

Theme: What we believe about God

"As I was walking through town and carefully observing your objects of worship, I even found an altar with this inscription: 'To an unknown God.' What you worship as unknown, I now proclaim to you. God, who made the world and everything in it, is Lord of heaven and earth. He doesn't live in temples made with human hands. Nor is God served by human hands, as though he needed something, since he is the one who gives life, breath, and everything else. From one person God created every human nation to live on the whole earth, having determined their appointed times and the boundaries of their lands. God made the nations so they would seek him, perhaps even reach out to him and find him. In fact, God isn't far away from any of us. In God we live, move, and exist. As some of your own poets said, 'We are his offspring.'"

—**Acts 17:23-28**

Three Simple Questions

As the youth arrive, ask them to list on a markerboard any Christian denominations or traditions they are familiar with. These could include United Methodist, Catholic, Presbyterian, Baptist, Lutheran, Eastern Orthodox, and so on. When most of the youth are present and have contributed, look over the list.

Ask:

- Why, do you think, are there so many different types of Christians?

Say: "Our Christian faith raises a lot of questions—about God, about people, about love and sin and life and death. Some of these questions are difficult to answer, and disagreements about how to answer them have caused divisions in the church."

Invite the youth to name some of the tough questions that Christians must answer. Examples include: How do we know if something is sinful? What happens when we take Holy Communion? or, When and how should someone be baptized?

If time permits, divide the youth into groups of 3 or 4 and ask each group to compile a list of tough questions that cause disagreement among Christians. They can record these under "Not-So-Simple Questions" in the student book on page 6. Give the groups a few minutes to work, then invite each group to read aloud its list of questions. List each group's questions on a markerboard.

Now explain that, while there are millions of questions that Christians debate and seek to answer, this study will focus on three simple—but essential—questions: Who is God? Who am I? and Who are we together? By asking these three questions, we will learn a lot about ourselves, about God, and about our faith.

The Mystery Question: Who Is God?

Investigating a question, particularly one as big as the "Who is God?" question, often leads to more questions. As a group take time to talk about what youth already know about God. It is important to listen to everyone's response and to offer ideas and thoughts that encourage more conversation. It is also important to remember that people speak from their personal experiences and describe God using their own words. The youth might say something like: "God is the Creator of the universe because that's what my parents told me"; or "God is the king of the world and controls the way we live our lives"; or "God is the big man in the sky who dishes out blessings and curses to people who are good or bad." Don't correct the youth or try to influence their answers.

Ask volunteers to read aloud Acts 17:23-28, printed on page 6 in the student book. Explain that, in this Scripture, the apostle Paul is in Athens. Athens was a cosmopolitan city and was home to people from all over the Roman world. As a result the city was full of idols and altars to all sorts of gods. Paul, wanting to tell the Athenians about Christ, noticed an altar "To an unknown God." He explained that the God they were seeking was the God revealed in Christ. Paul then went on to describe God to the people of Athens, quoting familiar Greek poets so that they would better understand who God is and how God was at work among them.

Paul was answering the question, "Who is God?" Tell your youth that, during this week and next, they will discuss this same question.

"We Name Our Gods"

Rueben Job in *Three Simple Questions* suggests that we name God by our actions—or how we choose to live. Instruct the youth to turn to "We Name Our Gods" on page 7 of the student book.

Ask youth to recall public figures who live for all to see and to identify some of the "gods" that these people name by their actions. These gods could include money, athletic ability, good looks, fashion, and so on.

Instruct youth to complete the first portion of the "We Name Our Gods" activity by naming three public people and the "gods" that they name. Explain that they don't need to name specific people but can instead name types of people, such as professional athlete, politician, or movie star.

Give the youth plenty of time to work, then invite volunteers to call out some of the examples they've listed. Be clear that the point of this activity is not to say that famous people worship false gods. Instead, the purpose is to think about what our actions say about our priorities and the "gods" we worship.

Then ask: "What gods do you name through your actions?"

Ask the youth to return to the "We Name Our Gods" activity and complete the second portion on page 8 by listing people in their lives whose actions "name" the God who is revealed in Christ. Encourage the youth to name specific people and to identify characteristics of God that these people reveal (*love, sacrifice, compassion, patience, creativity, and so on*).

Again, give the youth several minutes to work, then invite volunteers to tell who they listed and what characteristics of God these people reveal.

Then ask: "What do we believe about God?"

Collect and provide statements from your congregation and/or denomination that describe who God is.

Search the Scriptures

Ask the youth to turn to page 9 in the student book. Assign youth to pairs or groups of three and ask them to complete "Search the Scriptures" by finding and reading the Scriptures listed, then making notes about what each Scripture says about how we reveal God through our actions.

The Scriptures are:

- **Deuteronomy 30:15-20** (God gives us a choice.)
- **Mark 12:29-31** (Jesus teaches the greatest commandments.)
- **John 4:24** (God is spirit and truth.)
- **Romans 5:1-5** (Through Christ we have peace and hope.)
- **Ephesians 4:1-6** (Live as people worthy of the call we received from God.)
- **1 John 4:11-16** (We should love one another as God has loved us.)

Week One Investigation

Tell the youth to take home their student books and, during the coming week, investigate the three clues provided in "Week One Investigation" on pages 10–12 of the student book.

They should find and document examples of each clue. For example, for Clue No. 1: "God belongs to no one but who gives love, grace, and blessing to everyone," youth should find someone who offers love, grace, and blessings to whomever he or she sees. The youth could write a short paragraph about this person in the student book; they could take a picture of this person; or they could make a short video featuring this person. They should also find a Scripture verse that supports each clue and record it in the student book. To find such a Scripture, they could use a concordance, or they could use one of the many services available on the Internet.

As an alternative to allowing the youth to take home their student books, you could send the clues as text messages, one at a time, throughout the week. The youth could respond, sending text messages about the people and Scriptures they find.

The three clues for this activity are:

- **Clue No. 1:** "God who belongs to no one but who gives love, grace, and blessing to everyone." (*Three Simple Questions*, page 17)

- **Clue No. 2:** "God of radical mercy, justice, and love. ...The God of love is not simply 'nice' but has an edge, a passion for justice." (*Three Simple Questions*, page 17; *The Heart of Christianity*, page 77)

- **Clue No. 3:** "Your kingdom come." (*Three Simple Questions*, page 18)

Prayer for Focus

Close with the prayer on the following page and on page 14 of the student book.

Creator God, author of all that is and lover of all that you have made, deepen our awareness of your mighty acts past and present and your constant presence with us every moment of our existence. Invade our minds, senses, and hearts like a quiet sunrise, a refreshing rain, a beautiful bouquet, a commanding voice, a trusted companion, and a loving touch—because we want to know you and remember who you are with every breath we take.

By the power of your grace, transform us more and more until we become beautiful reflections of your presence and likeness in all that we do and are, as we offer all that we are and have to you in the Name and Spirit of Christ. Amen.

—**Rueben Job,** *Three Simple Questions*

Reading Assignment (Optional)

If possible, make available one copy of *Three Simple Questions,* by Rueben Job, for each youth. Ask the youth to read the chapter, "Who Is God?" (pages 11–32) in the coming week. Encourage them to think about the following questions as they read. (These questions are printed on pages 13–14 of the student book.)

- Rueben Job says that we name our gods by our words and actions. What are some of the gods that you name by your actions?
- What does it mean for God to be a God of love?
- What does it mean for God to be a God of justice?
- How can we know who God is?
- What do we know about God from the person of Jesus?
- What do we know about God from the person of the Holy Spirit?

Session

Question 1: Who Is God?
Part 2

Theme: We know God through the persons of Jesus and the Holy Spirit

> Despite our tendency to sometimes follow lesser gods, we know that, as Christians, the God we profess to follow is a particular God. We know that the call of Jesus to follow him is a call to follow the God he lovingly called *Abba* and to whom he fully gave his own life.
> **—Rueben Job,** *Three Simple Questions*

Who Is Jesus? Who Is the Holy Spirit?

This session focuses on Jesus and begins by taking a look at the Trinity. As you prepare for this session, think about how you understand the triune God. Reflect on these questions:

- Who is Jesus?
- Who is God the Father, or Creator?
- Who is the Holy Spirit?

Begin the session by saying: "This week we will continue our discussion of the question, 'Who is God?' by asking, 'Who is Jesus?' But before we talk about Jesus, we need to understand the Trinity. We believe in one God in three persons. The three persons of the Trinity are God the Father, or Creator; God the Son; and God the Holy Spirit. All three persons of the Trinity are equally important, but the person of Jesus gives us the clearest picture of who God is."

Discuss the following questions:

- What stories of Jesus (if any) do you remember learning as a child?
- Based on what you know about Jesus, how would you describe him?
- What words or images come to mind when you think of Jesus?
- Based on what you know of the Holy Spirit, how would you describe the Holy Spirit?
- How have you experienced the Holy Spirit? (If the youth have trouble identifying ways that they have experienced the Holy Spirit, ask them if they've ever felt God leading them to do something or nudging them in a certain direction; ask if they've ever felt peace and comfort during a difficult time.)

Reading Assignment (Optional)

If your group completed the optional reading assignment (the "Who Is God?" chapter of *Three Simple Questions*), begin by asking the youth to give their impressions of the reading and to name some of the key points that the author, Rueben Job, makes in this chapter. Then discuss the questions below, which the youth were asked to think about while reading:

- Rueben Job says that we name our gods by our words and actions. What are some of the gods that you name by your actions?
- What does it mean for God to be a God of love?
- What does it mean for God to be a God of justice?
- How can we know who God is?
- What do we know about God from the person of Jesus?
- What do we know about God from the person of the Holy Spirit?

Search the Scriptures

Ask the youth to turn to page 16 in the student book. Assign youth to pairs or groups of three and ask them to complete "Search the Scriptures" by finding and reading the Scriptures listed, determining whether each one describes Jesus or the Holy Spirit, then making notes about what each Scripture says about Jesus or the Holy Spirit.

The Scriptures are:

- **Matthew 2:1-12** (The magi visit Jesus.)
- **Matthew 16:13-16** (Peter declares Jesus the Messiah.)
- **Luke 8:22-25** (Jesus calms the sea.)
- **John 3:34-35** (The Father loves and gives everything to the Son.)
- **John 14:9-10** (Whoever has seen Jesus has seen the Father.)
- **John 14:25-26** (God will send the Holy Spirit to teach us.)
- **Acts 2:1-13** (The Holy Spirit is poured out at Pentecost.)
- **Galatians 5:16-17, 22-23** (When the Spirit guides us, we bear fruit.)
- **Philippians 2:5-11** (Jesus humbled himself and became a servant.)

The Trinity, Illustrated

Give each youth one sheet of paper and set out markers, colored pencils, and/or other art supplies. Ask the youth to imagine that a group of people who know nothing about Jesus or the Holy Spirit has asked them to explain Jesus and the Holy Spirit using only a single sheet of paper. Instruct the youth to describe Jesus on one side of the paper and the Holy Spirit on the other. Encourage them to use both words and images and to draw from the Scriptures they read in "Search the Scriptures" (above).

Give the youth several minutes to work, then invite volunteers to present their descriptions to the group.

Ask:

- What do your descriptions of Jesus and the Holy Spirit tell people about God?

Week Two Investigation

As you did last week, ask the youth to take home their student books and, during the coming week, investigate the three clues provided in "Week Two Investigation" on pages 17–19 of the student book.

Youth should find and document examples of each clue. For example, for Clue No. 1, "Jesus reminds us that love is our connection to him and his beloved Abba," youth should find an example of one way in which we stay connected to God through love. The youth could write a short paragraph about how they or someone they know shows love for God, possibly by loving others. They could also take a picture and/or make a short video illustrating how love connects us to God. They should also find a Scripture verse that supports each clue and record it in the student book. To find such a Scripture, they could use a concordance, or they could use one of the many services available on the Internet.

As an alternative to asking the youth to take home the student book, you could send the clues as text messages, one at a time, throughout the week. The youth could respond, sending text messages about the people and Scriptures they find.

The three clues for this activity are:

- **Clue No. 1:** "Jesus reminds us that love is our connection to him and his beloved Abba." (*Three Simple Questions*, page 24)

- **Clue No. 2:** "The apostle Paul reminds us that we are to imitate this God of love in our own lives." (*Three Simple Questions*, page 24)

- **Clue No. 3:** "Heaven is declaring God's glory; the sky is proclaiming his handiwork. One day gushes the news to the next, and one night informs another what needs to be known. Of course, there's no speech, no words—their voices can't be heard—but their sound extends throughout the world; their words reach the ends of the earth" (Psalm 19:1-4).

Prayer for Focus

Hand out sheets of paper and invite the youth to spend a few minutes writing a prayer of thanksgiving. As the youth write, take time to write your own prayer of thanksgiving in the space below. Invite one or more volunteers to read aloud their prayers as a group closing prayer. If youth are slow to volunteer to read their prayers, read your prayer aloud to begin.

Everything that came from Jesus's lips worked like a magnifying glass to focus human awareness on the two most important facts about life: God's overwhelming love of humanity, and the need for people to accept that love and let it flow through them in the way water passes without obstruction through a sea anemone.
—**Huston Smith,** *The Soul of Christianity* **(Harper SanFrancisco, 2005)**

When we face
darkness in our lives,
we know that God is
present and that God's
light will cut through
the darkness.

Question 2

Who Am I?
Introduction

> We are children of the light, children of God; and when we claim our full inheritance as children of God, we are able to see clearly and to know in the depth of our being that when we look at another human being, we are looking at a sister or brother who is God's beloved child, just as we are.
>
> **—Rueben Job,** *Three Simple Questions*

In the first two sessions we asked the question, "Who is God?" We discovered that how we answer this seemingly simple question has a big impact on what we believe and how we live as Christians. It also affects our understanding of who we are. This brings us to the second question: "Who am I?"

Like "Who is God?" the question "Who am I?" seems simple on its surface, but answering it can be quite challenging. We live in a world "darkened by confusion, deception, and dysfunction" (*Three Simple Questions*, page 40). Amid all this darkness, it's easy to forget who we are. We can get caught up in the labels that other people attach to us; and we can be overwhelmed by temptation to participate in the darkness.

As children of God and followers of Christ, we are not people of darkness. We are people of the light. As each of us is God's beloved creation, God calls us to treat others as God's beloved creation also, reflecting the light of Christ. We are who we are because of whose we are. And we demonstrate who we are by the way we live and love.

Youth and the Question

Every teenager struggles to answer the question, "Who am I?" Adolescence is a time when we identify ourselves apart from our parents and make decisions about who we are and who we are not.

Some youth may have quick answers to the question, "Who am I?" Some may respond with pride, saying: "I am an A+ student" or "I am so-and-so's girlfriend or boyfriend" or "I am the starting point guard on the varsity basketball team" or "I play sax in the jazz band." You fill in the blank. Youth tend to define themselves in the ways that the world defines them. If their friends or the culture around them values athletic ability or grades or relationship status, they will describe themselves according to these values.

That said, young people are still growing, maturing, and changing. They are not set in their ways. They are willing to explore new possibilities and take on new challenges. Teens may have an answer to the question, "Who am I?"—but this answer isn't set in stone. What greater gift can we give youth than to help them explore the question more deeply?

As Christians we believe that who we are is tied to who God is. Question 2 is inseparable from Question 1. In the first session of this study, youth considered the "gods" they name by their words and actions. When we choose to name the God who is revealed in Christ and the Holy Spirit, the question, "Who am I?" becomes "Who am I as a child of God?"

Teaching These Sessions

Question 2: Who Am I? Part 1

This first of the two "Who Am I?" sessions looks at the darkness that surrounds us and makes it difficult for us to see clearly who we are and whom God calls us to be. In this session, youth will talk about the darkness they encounter; they will consider how they contribute to or participate in this darkness; and they will identify ways in which they can reflect God's light.

When you teach this lesson, be clear that all people sometimes contribute to darkness. As Paul writes in Romans 3:23: "All have sinned and fall short of God's glory." Youth also need to understand that, by God's grace through Christ, we are forgiven. While it's important that youth are aware

24

of the ways in which they participate in darkness, the purpose of this lesson is not to make them feel guilty. Instead youth should look for ways that they can live out their identities as God's children and people of the light.

Question 2: Who Am I? Part 2

The second session takes a close look at our identities as beloved children of God. Youth will hear the good news that God created them, claims them, and loves them. They will learn about God's grace and how God's grace is at work throughout our lives.

You will have the option, as part of this session, to include a ritual in which participants remember and reaffirm their baptism. While the instructions for the ritual take into consideration youth who have not yet been baptized, if many of your youth have not been baptized, this ritual may not be appropriate. Instead you could talk with the youth about baptism as an initiation into the church and an identifier of who we are as God's children. Consult baptismal resources available through your congregation or denomination or a member of your pastoral staff.

Basic Supplies for This Study

The following supplies will be used frequently throughout this study, so they will not be listed in the supplies for each activity:

- Bibles
- Student books
- Pens or pencils
- Markerboard and markers
- Copy of *Three Simple Questions,* by Rueben Job, for each youth (optional)

God created each one of
us with a purpose, and
God has equipped us for
that purpose. Our job is
to discover who we are
in the light of God.

Session

Question 2: Who Am I?
Part 1

Theme: Living in darkness

> When God began to create the heavens and the earth—the earth was without shape or form, it was dark over the deep sea, and God's wind swept over the waters—God said, "Let there be light." And so light appeared. God saw how good the light was. God separated the light from the darkness.
>
> **—Genesis 1:1-4**

Light in the Darkness

Beforehand, prepare your meeting room so that it will be as dark as possible. Cover windows and remove any obstacles that would make walking around in the dark treacherous. If you want to go the extra mile, use a fog machine to help create an especially dark and dreary space.

Place glow sticks throughout the room. Put some of the glow sticks in places where the youth might expect to find them, such as near lamps or by the door. Place others in illogical places where youth might not expect to find them. (The idea is that the first persons to find the easily located glow sticks can help the other persons uncover the harder-to-find glow sticks.) Then turn out all the lights.

Supplies
- one glow stick per student (the kind that don't light up until you bend them)

As the youth arrive, challenge each one to find a glow stick. You and the other adults will need to monitor the situation to make sure that everyone stays safe. One by one, as the glow sticks are found and lit, light will shine out of the darkness and the youth will be able to see more clearly.

The Mystery Question: What Is It Like to Be in Darkness?

Say: "This week we will look at our world and what it's like to be in darkness."

Ask:

- Where do you see darkness in our world?

Say: "Often when we think of darkness, we think of wickedness and evil. But, as we experienced in the opening activity, darkness can also involve not seeing things clearly. And darkness isn't always bad. Without darkness we wouldn't know light. Consider that God made both the day and the night."

Ask a volunteer to read aloud Genesis 1:1-4.

Then say: "We believe that God created all things and that God declared all things good, even the darkness. We also believe that God is present with us in the darkness."

Ask:

- How did you find the glow sticks in our opening activity?

Say: "You knew that, even though the room was dark, there was light to be found. The same is true when we face darkness in our lives. We know that God is present and that God's light will cut through the darkness. Once some of you found glow sticks, you were able to help one another find more. The same is true of the light of Christ. When one of us discovers the light of Christ, we share that light with others, and the light continues to grow."

Ask:

- Where have you seen the light of Christ in times of darkness?
- How have you shared this light with others?

Say: "Here's the deal: God didn't create good people and bad people in this world. God created *all* people. God has given us the gift of free will, and we can choose to live in darkness or to live in the light. Many people have chosen to live in darkness, either because of circumstances created by others or circumstances created by themselves. Today we'll investigate the darkness in our world and how we can shine a light through that darkness."

Search the Scriptures

Ask the youth to turn to page 20 in the student book. Assign them to pairs or groups of three and ask them to complete "Search the Scriptures" by looking up the verses listed, selecting two Scriptures that tell how God was present amid darkness, and completing the appropriate blanks.

Give youth plenty of time to work, then invite each group to name the Scriptures it selected and what it wrote about those Scriptures.

The Scriptures are:

- **Isaiah 42:16** (God turned darkness into light.)
- **Isaiah 60:2** (The Lord shines on the earth's darkness.)
- **Matthew 5:14-16** (Let your light shine before others.)
- **Luke 1:67-79** (Zechariah prophesied about Jesus.)
- **John 1:1-5** (Jesus is the light who shines through the darkness.)
- **John 8:12** (Jesus is the light of the world.)
- **Romans 13:11-14** (Behave as people who live in the light.)

Taking Responsibility

Say: "Often our first reaction when we encounter darkness is to blame someone, or even to blame God. It's much more difficult for us to consider how we might be contributing to the darkness or to find ways to shine the light of Christ."

Invite the youth to spend a few minutes in silence, thinking about ways they contribute to darkness. Perhaps they participate in gossip or bully their peers; maybe they have stolen something or cheated on a test. Ask them to list beneath "Taking Responsibility," on page 22 in the student book, one or two ways in which they have added to darkness. (For the sake of privacy, instead of writing in the student book, youth may write on slips of paper and keep them in their wallets, purses, or Bibles.)

Then ask the youth to reflect on ways they can add to the light. This could include participation in mission and service ministries; going out of their way to encourage friends and peers; befriending someone who is new to the school or church; and so on. Ask them to list in the student book one or two ways in which they can reflect the light of Christ. Do not ask anyone to say aloud what he or she has written.

Week Three Investigation

As you did last week, ask the youth to take home their student books and, during the coming week, investigate the three clues provided in "Week Three Investigation" on pages 23–25 of the student book.

As an alternative to youth taking home their student books, you could send the clues as text messages, one at a time, throughout the week. The youth could respond, sending text messages about the people and Scriptures they find.

- **Clue No. 1:** "God sent Jesus, the Word, into our dark world to bring life, light, hope, healing, and peace. Yet today much of the world still lies in darkness." (*Three Simple Questions*, page 39)

- **Clue No. 2:** "May the God of hope fill you with all joy and peace in faith so that you overflow with hope by the power of the Holy Spirit. My brothers and sisters, I myself am convinced that you yourselves are full of goodness, filled with all knowledge, and are able to teach each other" (Romans 15:13-14).

- **Clue No. 3:** "In this world darkened by confusion, deception, and dysfunction, it is easy to forget who we are." (*Three Simple Questions*, page 40)

We are closest to God in the darkness ....

—Madeleine L'Engle

Prayer for Focus

Close with the Serenity Prayer on page 27 of the student book:

God, grant me the serenity to accept the things I cannot change,
Courage to change the things I can,
And wisdom to know the difference. Amen.

—Reinhold Niebuhr

Reading Assignment (Optional)

If possible, provide one copy of *Three Simple Questions,* by Rueben Job, for each youth. Ask the youth to read the chapter "Who Am I?" (pages 35–49) during the coming week. Encourage them to think about the following questions as they read. (These questions are printed on page 26–27 of the student book).

- What does it mean for our world to be in darkness? How do you experience darkness in your life?
- How does darkness affect you? How do you contribute to the darkness?
- How do you identify yourself? What words and descriptions do you use?
- How do other people identify you? What words and descriptions do they use?
- What does it mean to be a child of God?
- How do we live as children of God?
- How does prayer help us remember who we are as children of God?
- How can you make daily prayer a habit, if it isn't already?

When the priests left the holy place, the cloud filled the LORD's temple, and the priests were unable to carry out their duties due to the cloud because the LORD's glory filled the LORD's temple. Then Solomon said, "The LORD said that he would live in a dark cloud, but I have indeed built you a lofty temple as a place where you can live forever."

—1 Kings 8:10-13

Question 2: Who Am I?
Part 2

Theme: Living as beloved children of God

> God created humanity in God's own image, in the divine image God created them, male and female God created them.
>
> **—Genesis 1:27**

We Are Beloved Children of God

Beforehand, set out the art supplies and write the statement, *We are beloved children of God*, on a markerboard.

As the youth arrive, invite them to create a painting that illustrates what it means to be a beloved child of God. This painting can show blessings that we receive as God's children, how we live as God's children, or how we show or experience God's love. The painting can be realistic or abstract. Try to avoid giving too many suggestions; leave the activity open to interpretation.

Supplies
- Small canvases or sheets of paper
- Paint
- Paint brushes

Give the youth plenty of time to work on their paintings. Then invite them to talk about what they painted and how their paintings show what it means to be a beloved child of God.

The Mystery Question: Why Am I Here?

Say: "At some point in our lives, all of us ask, 'Who am I?' or 'Why do I exist?' or 'Why am I here?' As we discussed in the previous session, people often label us and sometimes we label ourselves. But no label is more important than the label *child of God*."

Ask:

- What, do you think, does it mean to be a child of God?

Say: "Today we're going to investigate what the label *child of God* truly means. With that in mind, let's see how our paintings look using different types of light."

Look at the paintings under each type of light. For each ask:

- How do your paintings look different under this light?
- Do you think that your paintings look better or worse? Why?

Provide a variety of light sources:
- Florescent
- Incandescent
- natural sunlight
- colored light
- black light

Supplies

Then say: "We all painted very different images to represent 'beloved child of God.' In some types of light, the images looked just as we intended them to look. In other types of light, they looked different—maybe even distorted. But, for each of us, our painting is our painting, whether other people like it or not and regardless of what sort of light is used."

Ask the youth to think about something that they have spent a great deal of time creating or working on and that they value and of which they claim ownership. Ask:

- What did you think of the item you created?
- How did you feel about it when it was complete?
- Did others feel the same way that you felt?

Then say: "God created each and every one of us. God claims all of us as valuable creations. God loves us and has a vision for our lives. God created each one of us with a purpose, and God has equipped us for that purpose. Our job is to discover who we are in the light of God."

Reading Assignment (Optional)

If your group did the optional reading assignment (the "Who Am I?" chapter of *Three Simple Questions*), begin by asking the youth to give their impressions of the reading and to name some of the key points that

33

the author, Rueben Job, makes in this chapter. Then discuss the following questions that youth were asked to consider:

- What does it mean for our world to be in darkness? How do you experience darkness in your life?
- How does darkness affect you? How do you contribute to the darkness?
- How do you identify yourself? What words and descriptions do you use?
- How do other people identify you? What words and descriptions do they use?
- What does it mean to be a child of God?
- How do we live as children of God?
- How does prayer help us remember who we are as children of God?
- How can you make prayer a daily habit, if it isn't already?

Search the Scriptures

Ask the youth to turn to page 28 in the student book. Assign them to pairs or groups of three and ask them to complete "Search the Scriptures" by finding and reading the verses listed, each of which deals with a parent-child relationship, and describing the relationship in each Scripture.

Give youth plenty of time to work, then invite each group to name the Scriptures it selected and tell what it wrote about those Scriptures.

The Scriptures are:

- **Genesis 27:1-29**
- **Ruth 1:1-18**
- **1 Samuel 19:1-7**
- **Luke 15:11-24**
- **Luke 15:25-32**

Then ask:

- What do these Scriptures tell us about what it means to be a child of God?
- How is our parent-child relationship with God similar to and different from the relationships you read about in these Scriptures?

The Three Movements of Grace

Say: "Grace is a gift from God. It is not something we earn. It is something that God makes available to us through the death and resurrection of Christ. Through grace, God saves us from sin and death." Ask the youth to talk about what they know about grace.

Then say: "We experience God's grace even before we are aware of God. John Wesley, the founder of Methodism, referred to this type of grace as *prevenient grace.* An infant doesn't know that her parents are offering her love. She only knows that she has basic needs. She cries when she is hungry, thirsty, uncomfortable because of a dirty diaper, too hot, or too cold. She can't say, 'Thank you.' She just knows that someone or something met her needs. That's like prevenient grace. Even before we know who God is or that we need God's grace, God is there, watching over us and nudging us in the right direction."

35

Ask:

- When were you first aware of God? How, do you think, was God at work in your life even before you were aware of God?

Then say: "As we grow up, we realize that we have free will. As we become aware of God and God's love for us, we can use our freedom to claim God's love. John Wesley called this type of grace, which allows us to respond to God's love, *justifying grace*. Through justifying grace, we identify ourselves as children of God, express a desire for a transformed life, and have assurance that our sins are forgiven.

"Once we have this assurance, we spend the rest of our life growing in love of God and neighbor. We grow by practicing our faith and staying connected to God. This grace, which enables us to grow in faith, is called *sanctifying grace*."

Ask:

- In what ways can you practice your faith and stay connected to God? (*prayer, worship, Holy Communion, acts of compassion, acts of justice, Bible study, and so forth*)

Say: "As we grow in grace, we will continue to slip up and make mistakes. But God's grace covers us when we sin. We know that we are forgiven, and God's grace gives us the strength to turn away from our sin and head in a new direction."

Remember Your Baptism (Optional)

In *Three Simple Questions* Rueben Job tells us that, whenever the reformer Martin Luther felt dismayed, he would remember his baptism. Baptism—a sacrament ordained by Jesus himself—is an important way that Christians throughout history have identified themselves as Christ's followers. One way that Christians can answer the question, "Who am I?" is to remember or reaffirm our individual baptisms.

Supplies
- A pitcher of water
- A water basin filled with a supply of small stones, marbles, or beads (one per student)

Say a prayer of blessing over the water. Your congregation or denomination may have resources for reaffirmation of baptism services.

Then remind those in the group who were baptized that, upon baptism, they received a new name—the name of Christ. Also remind them that baptism is the formal entry into the body of Christ, the church. Then pour the water into the basin.

Invite participants who have been baptized to come to the water basin and touch the water. As each person touches the water, use the water to make the sign of the cross on his or her forehead (much like you would make the sign of the cross with ashes on Ash Wednesday); and say to him or her, "Remember your baptism and be thankful."

Invite each person to take a small stone, marble, or bead from the basin as a reminder of their reaffirmation and remembrance of baptism.

Invite participants who have not yet been baptized to also come forward to receive a blessing in anticipation of their baptism. Say to these persons, "Anticipate your baptism and be thankful."

Note: Be clear that this is not a service of baptism. It is a ritual and a blessing, but it is not a sacrament.

Option: If all of the participants have been baptized, and if they are comfortable doing so, allow them to pair up and invite partners to make the sign of the cross on each other's foreheads, saying, "Remember your baptism and be thankful."

Week Four Investigation

As you did last week, ask the youth to take home their student books and, during the coming week, investigate the three clues provided in "Week Four Investigation" on pages 30–32 of the student book.

As an alternative to youth taking home their student books, you could send the clues as text messages, one at a time, throughout the week. The youth could respond, sending text messages about the people and Scriptures they find.

The three clues for this activity are:

- **Clue No. 1:** "We rise from prayer transformed because we have been intimately involved with the One who not only gives us life but also transforms our lives while leading us further and further into that grand design that God has for each of us." (*Three Simple Questions*, page 46)

- **Clue No. 2:** "Whenever he was troubled or dismayed, the reformer Martin Luther would remember his baptism. ... Those familiar with Luther's custom have found a practice of their own to remind themselves who they are, and it is something that can be practiced by all Christians. The practice is simply to speak your own name, put your fingers to your head, and repeat, 'Remember who you are.' As you do this, remember your baptism and affirm that you are a beloved child of God. Then offer a prayer of thanks." (*Three Simple Questions*, page 48)

- **Clue No. 3:** Chandler English, an eighth grader in Athens, Georgia, wrote the following thoughts on Exodus 3:14: "God said to Moses, 'I Am Who I Am.' This is the Bible verse that I live by, because I've grown up being asked by many classmates, 'Why are you so different?' or 'Why can't you just act normal for once?' If I had the biblical knowledge I have now, I could've just said, 'Exodus 3:14: "I Am Who I Am."'"

Prayer for Focus

Close with the prayer below from *Three Simple Questions* (page 49), which is also found on page 29 of the student book.

Loving God, Remind me often today where I find my identity. May I never forget that I am your beloved child. May I listen for and hear your faintest whisper, feel your slightest touch, respond quickly to your call, yield to your word of correction, rejoice in your companionship, and serve you faithfully all the days of my life.

Thank you for hearing my prayers and accepting my life. I offer them to you as completely as I can in the Name and Spirit of Jesus Christ. Amen.

—Rueben Job, *Three Simple Questions*

Notes

Means of grace are
spiritual practices
through which we
open ourselves to
God's grace. Means
of grace bring us
closer to God and
bring us closer
together as a family.

Question 3

Who Are We Together?
Introduction

> Living in community is not easy. Sometimes we are able to live together faithfully only when we remember that God is there with us, and that it is God's love that binds us together into the body of Christ.
> —**Rueben Job,** *Three Simple Questions*

So far, we've asked, "Who is God?" and "Who am I?" We've learned about God from the person of Jesus and from the Holy Spirit, who lives in us and among us today. And we've discussed who we are as God's children and what it means to live as a child of God.

But faith is not a solitary exercise. Jesus calls us to be a church, a community of believers. We are not only to love God but also to love our fellow human beings, including enemies and strangers. Loving every person we encounter and treating every person as a member of our family is no easy task. Nor is living together with others in a community of faith. Being a member of God's family means seeing people differently and being willing to make sacrifices on behalf of our brothers and sisters.

Living together with our many brothers and sisters takes practice. Fortunately there are plenty of ways that we can practice our faith. These practices—which include prayer, worship, Bible study, and acts of mercy—are called *means of grace*. Means of grace open us to God's grace and empower us to live together in love.

41

Youth and the Question

The teenage brain is still developing. Young adolescents, for example, often struggle with abstract thinking and nuance. As they mature they begin to notice the shades of gray between the white and the black.

Empathy—the ability to identify with the feelings and needs of others—is a trait that continues to develop into adulthood. Thus, leading teens to think beyond their personal needs and desires can be quite a challenge.

Jesus, citing Leviticus 19:18, commands us to love our neighbors as ourselves (see Mark 12:29-31). Youth need to understand what Jesus means when he says the word *neighbor*. Adolescents are social beings, but they often enter relationships for selfish reasons or for mutual gratification. Many aren't inclined to enter relationships that require sacrifice and provide no obvious benefits. But that's what loving neighbors requires.

Youth also need to understand that all human beings—including enemies and people they don't know—are their neighbors and are God's beloved creations. Every person we encounter is part of our human family and is deserving of our love and compassion.

Who are we together? We're neighbors. And we're family.

Teaching These Sessions

Question 3: Who Are We Together? Part 1

This first session is all about family. Often when we hear the word *family*, we think of people who are related to us by blood or marriage. But, as we learned in the "Who Am I?" sessions, we are children of God. And God's family is much bigger than the group of people who gathers around our kitchen table or gets together at holidays. This session challenges youth to think of all people as family members.

As you teach, challenge the youth to think about any prejudices that keep them from loving others. Also help them identify ways that they can treat every person they encounter as a brother or sister.

Question 3: Who Are We Together? Part 2

The second session looks at our family of faith, the church. It looks at ways that our family teaches important lessons to younger generations. These faith lessons originated with Jesus himself.

This session also introduces the concept of *means of grace*—spiritual practices through which we open ourselves to God's grace. These practices include prayer, worship, devotion, acts of mercy, reading and studying Scripture, and any other way in which we practice our faith and express our love for God and neighbor. Means of grace bring us closer to God and bring us closer together as a family.

Basic Supplies for This Study

The following supplies will be used frequently throughout this study, so they will not be listed in the supplies for each activity:

- Bibles
- Student books
- Paper
- Pens or pencils
- Markerboard and/or large sheets of paper
- Broad-tip markers
- Copy of *Three Simple Questions,* by Rueben Job, for each youth (optional)

How does being
faithful to Christ
affect how we
live together as
a Christian
community?

Session

Question 3:
Who Are We Together?
Part 1

Theme: Seeing through the eyes of God

Peter said, "I really am learning that God doesn't show partiality to one group of people over another. Rather, in every nation, whoever worships him and does what is right is acceptable to him. This is the message of peace he sent to the Israelites by proclaiming the good news through Jesus Christ: He is Lord of all!

—Acts 10:34-36

The Biblical Family Tree

Read aloud Genesis 12:1-3. Say: "God promised Abraham and Sarah—who were then known as Abram and Sarai—that their descendents would become a great nation and a blessing to all the nations on earth."

Divide the youth into groups of three or four and ask the groups to create a family tree for Abraham and Sarah using the Scriptures on page 33 of the student book. Youth may draw the family tree on paper or create one by writing names on cards, taping the cards to the wall, and connecting the cards with pieces of string.

Give the groups several minutes to work. Then look over their family trees. Say, "We encounter Abraham's descendents throughout the Old and New Testaments." Invite the youth to turn to Matthew 1:1-17, the genealogy of Jesus. Point out that Matthew traces Jesus' lineage back through King David and all the way to Abraham. The connection between Jesus is important because God had promised David that his "throne" would be "established forever." The Messiah being a descendent of David would be the ultimate fulfillment of this covenant. Point out other familiar names in the genealogy, such as Ruth and Solomon and King Josiah.

Now ask the youth to turn to Luke 3:23-38. Point out that this genealogy goes back even further, all the way to Adam. Explain that Luke's genealogy emphasizes that, while Jesus is fully God, he is also fully human and is connected to each and every one of us.

The Mystery Question:
What If We Considered Every Person Our Relative?

Ask:

- How are your relationships with family members different from your relationships with other people?

- How would your life be different if you treated everyone as if he or she were a member of your family? (Challenge youth to think about people they pass by who are homeless or stranded on the side of the road or people who sit alone in the school cafeteria.)

Option: Pair up youth. Instruct the persons in each pair to imagine that they don't know each other but have come into contact with each other for some reason. Maybe they are the drivers of two cars that just collided; maybe a teacher assigned them to be partners on a class project even though they'd never spoken before. Instruct the pairs to roleplay two situations, one in which the two people treat each other like family and one in which they treat each other like strangers.

Search the Scriptures

Ask the youth to turn to page 34 in the student book. Divide them into pairs or groups of three and ask them to complete "Search the Scriptures" by reading the Scriptures listed and identifying ways that Jesus reached out in love and compassion to someone unlike himself. Remind them that Jesus was Jewish, was raised in a Jewish family, and followed Jewish customs. Also remind them that Jews and Samaritans—who shared a similar heritage but disagreed on how to properly worship God—did not get along.

The Scriptures are:

- **Matthew 8:5-13** (Jesus heals a Roman centurion's servant.)
- **Luke 5:12-16** (Jesus heals a man with a skin disease.)
- **Luke 19:1-10** (Jesus invites Zacchaeus, a tax collector, into his home.)
- **John 4:4-42** (Jesus meets a Samaritan woman at the well.)

One Big Family

Ask volunteers to read aloud Acts 10:34-36 (page 33 in the student book), which Rueben Job refers to on page 59 of *Three Simple Questions*. Put this Scripture into context by explaining that Peter, like all of Jesus' first disciples, was Jewish. But God had called him to minister to a non-Jewish man who didn't follow Jewish customs. Peter was hesitant at first but eventually learned that God loves and works through people of all nations.

Ask the youth to name pairs of people or groups who are divided by their differences. (Examples would include Republicans and Democrats, Israelis and Palestinians, and so on.) List their examples on a markerboard. Once you have a good list, ask the youth to name things that people in each pair have in common.

Explain that, despite our differences, God calls us to be one body, the church. God also calls us to reach out to people of all backgrounds and to show them God's love.

Rueben Job, author of *Three Simple Questions*, wrote a book called *Three Simple Rules* that looked at John Wesley's three "General Rules." These rules are:

- Do no harm.
- Do good.
- Attend upon all the ordinances of God. (Job rephrases this rule as, "Stay in love with God."

Discuss why these three rules are important for living together in a Christian community and for reaching out to others. Explain that "Attend upon all the ordinances of God," or "Stay in love with God," means staying connected to God through spiritual practices such as prayer, worship, reading and studying the Bible, acts of mercy or service, taking Holy Communion, and so on.

Week Five Investigation

As you did last week, ask the youth to take home their student books and, during the coming week, investigate the three clues listed in "Week Five Investigation" on pages 35–37 of the student book.

- **Clue No. 1:** "Living in community is not easy. ... When we reflect thoughtfully on community, we quickly recognize that there are significant barriers preventing community in this noisy, violent, divided, and dysfunctional world." (*Three Simple Questions*, pages 54, 55)

- **Clue No. 2:** "Each of us is a member of this extended human family of God. God loves us as though each one of us was the only child of God in the world, just as God loves every other human being on the face of the earth." (*Three Simple Questions*, page 56)

- **Clue No. 3:** The parable of the good Samaritan (see Luke 10:29-37)

Prayer for Focus

Close with the prayer on the following page, which is also found on page 39 of the student book.

Reading Assignment (Optional)

If possible, provide a copy of *Three Simple Questions,* by Rueben Job, for each youth. Ask the youth in the coming week to read the chapter "Who Are We Together?" (pages 53–69). Tell them to think about the following questions as they read. (These questions are printed on pages 38–39 of the student book.)

- When have you been willing to do something that you wouldn't ordinarily do in order to spend more time with someone you love (whether a family member, a close friend, or a significant other)?
- What is most difficult about living together as a family or community?
- How are all human beings part of one family?
- What does it mean for all Christians to be part of one family?
- When do we, as Christians, fail to live together as a family?
- How do we fail to welcome people whom Jesus invites into the Christian community? How could we be more welcoming?
- What does it mean to live as a faithful follower of Jesus Christ?
- How does being faithful to Christ affect how we live together as a Christian community? How does it affect our relationships with the rest of the human family?

Precious Jesus, we give you thanks for the gift of life given to every human being on this planet. Help us to see one another the way you see us. Help us to see each person as a brother, sister, mother, father, aunt or uncle in our family. Help us to know that each person is your son or daughter and that your love for each of us is greater than we could ever imagine. You are our God and we are your people. Help us to live lives that make you proud to call us your children. In your holy name we pray, Amen!

—Rueben Job, *Three Simple Questions*

Session

Question 3: Who Are We Together?
Part 2

Theme: The church as a family of faith

> We cannot hope to follow God as revealed in Jesus if we never spend time together, allowing God to speak to us. On the other hand, the longer we intentionally live in God's presence—the longer we "hang out" with Jesus—the more like Jesus we become.
>
> **—Rueben Job,** *Three Simple Questions*

Family Time

As the youth arrive, ask them to come up with a definition of *family* and record this definition in the appropriate space on page 40 of the student book.

When most of the youth are present, invite volunteers to read aloud their definitions. Talk about similarities and differences among the definitions and discuss questions such as:

- Do people have to be related by blood or marriage to be part of a family? If not, what makes them a family?

The Mystery Question:
What Is Our Role in Our Faith Family?

Ask volunteers to read aloud 1 Corinthians 12:12-27. Talk with the youth about how the members of the church are part of one body, or family. Ask:

- Paul, in 1 Corinthians 12:12-27, talks about how the body is made up of many different parts, all of which are necessary. What are some of the different roles that people in our church family play? Why is each of these roles necessary?
- What gifts and abilities do you bring to the church family? How do you use these gifts to contribute to the family?

Say: "Family members contribute to the family in many different ways. But the one thing that family members should be able to count on from one another is love. Parents should show love to their children; older generations should show love to younger generations. The younger members of the family should then respond by showing love to others. Our challenge this week is to discover what our responsibility is as a member of God's faith family. How do we show love to God and to our brothers and sisters in Christ?"

Reading Assignment (Optional)

If your group did the optional reading assignment (the "Who Are We Together?" chapter of *Three Simple Questions*), begin by asking the youth to give their impressions of the reading and to name some of the key points that the author, Rueben Job, makes in this chapter. Then discuss the questions below that you asked youth to consider while reading:

- When have you been willing to do something that you wouldn't ordinarily do in order to spend more time with someone you love (whether a family member, a close friend, or a significant other)?
- What is most difficult about living together as a family or community?
- How are all human beings part of one family?
- What does it mean for all Christians to be part of one family?

51

- When do we, as Christians, fail to live together as a family?
- How do we fail to welcome people whom Jesus invites into the Christian community? How could we be more welcoming?
- What does it mean to live as a faithful follower of Jesus Christ?
- How does being faithful to Christ affect how we live together as a Christian community? How does it affect our relationships with the rest of the human family?

Search the Scriptures

Say: "Parents often tell children stories that teach moral lessons. Jesus did the same for the children of God. Jesus often used parables to get across these lessons."

Ask the youth to turn to page 41 in the student book. Divide them into pairs or groups of three and ask them to complete "Search the Scriptures" by looking up each of the parables listed, identifying the lesson it teaches, and naming a story they've heard that teaches a similar lesson.

The Scriptures are:

- **Matthew 18:21-35** (the parable of the unforgiving servant)
- **Matthew 20:1-16** (the parable of the workers in the vineyard)

- **Luke 13:18-21** (the parables of the mustard seed and yeast)
- **Luke 16:14-31** (the parable of the rich man and Lazarus)
- **Luke 19:11-27** (the parable of the unfaithful servant)

Means of Grace

Talk about any team sports or other team activities in which youth may participate, such as band, orchestra, or drama. Ask:

- How do you practice and prepare for these activities as an individual? How do you practice and prepare as a team?

Explain that, as members of the church, we are part of a team and we have a responsibility to practice our faith, both individually and as a team. Ask:

- How do we practice our faith as individuals? (*through prayer, devotional reading, acts of kindness, and so on*)
- How do we practice our faith as a team, or community? (*through worship, studying the Bible together, working together in mission and service, and so on*)
- How is practicing our faith similar to and different from practicing for other activities? (Talk about how we improve through practice, how practice brings a team together, how practice can sometimes be tedious and difficult, and how practice can help make things that were once difficult more manageable.)

Say: "John Wesley had a name for all of these ways that we practice our faith. He called them 'means of grace.' While God's grace is always available to all of us, these practices are ways that we open our arms to grace. Through means of grace we grow closer to God and one another. Means of grace are a way that we say, 'Yes,' to Christ and identify ourselves as his followers and his family."

As a part of the "Week Six Investigation," youth will make individual commitments to a means of grace using the challenge in the student book. A copy of this "30-Day Means of Grace Challenge" is included on pages 57–61 in this leader book.

But before youth work on individual commitments, as a group, determine one way that you will practice your faith together in the coming weeks.

Some ideas are a service project, meeting weekly for a Bible study or small-group devotion, or sitting together in worship each Sunday for a month. Record some ideas and brief plans for this commitment (along with possible dates, if necessary) in the space below. Be sure to encourage and remind youth to follow through on this commitment.

Week Six Investigation

Say: "Some people say that it takes thirty days for a habit to stick. For this week's Investigation, you will commit to practicing your faith each day for thirty days."

Direct the youth to the "30-Day Means of Grace Challenge" on pages 42–46 of the student book (also on pages 57–61 in this book). Each day suggests a prayer focus, a Scripture reading, and an act of mercy. Encourage the youth to do all three actions each day and to keep a record of what they've done. Consider assigning the youth accountability partners to encourage them in their progress.

Prayer for Focus

Close with the following prayer, which is also found on page 46 of the student book.

Tender Shepherd,
Gather us together as your flock, defend us from division, save us from sin,
Lead us in paths of righteousness, justice, peace, unity, and love,
Help us to discern wisely and well your will and way,
And grant us grace to follow faithfully wherever you may lead us, for we are yours and want to follow you alone.
Grant us grace to do so, we pray,
In the Name and Spirit of Jesus Christ, who taught us to pray . . . "Our Father . . . ." Amen.
     —Rueben Job, *Three Simple Questions*

Notes

30-Day Means of Grace Challenge

1. Sunday
Morning: Worship.
Evening: Read Genesis 1.
Mercy: Tell someone you love him or her.

2. Monday
Morning: Pray for the world.
Evening: Read Mark 1.
Mercy: Offer a kind word to a stranger.

3. Tuesday
Morning: Pray for the church.
Evening: Read Genesis 2.
Mercy: Clean up something for someone else.

4. Wednesday
Morning: Pray for your friends.
Evening: Read Mark 2.
Mercy: Offer a kind word to a friend.

5. Thursday
Morning: Pray for your family.
Evening: Read Genesis 3.
Mercy: Tell a parent you love him or her.

6. Friday
Morning: Pray for your community.
Evening: Read Mark 3.
Mercy: Don't say a single mean thing all day.

7. Saturday
Morning: Pray for your pastor.
Evening: Read Genesis 4.
Mercy: Help provide food for someone who is hungry.

8. Sunday
Morning: Worship.
Evening: Read Mark 4.
Mercy: Invite a friend to worship.

9. Monday
Morning: Pray for God's wisdom.
Evening: Read Genesis 5.
Mercy: Give a teacher a gift or a card.

10. Tuesday
Morning: Pray for God's hope.
Evening: Read Mark 5.
Mercy: Give clothes to someone who needs them.

11. Wednesday
Morning: Pray for God's love.
Evening: Read Genesis 6.
Mercy: Donate a Bible to someone who doesn't have one.

12. Thursday
Morning: Pray that you might have faith in others.
Evening: Read Mark 6.
Mercy: Offer someone forgiveness.

13. Friday
Morning: Pray for faith in yourself.
Evening: Read Genesis 7.
Mercy: Accept God's grace and forgiveness.

14. Saturday
Morning: Pray for your church's lay leader.
Evening: Read Mark 7.
Mercy: Write a note of encouragement to someone in
your congregation.

30-Day Means of Grace Challenge

15. Sunday

Morning: Worship.
Evening: Read Genesis 8.
Mercy: Invite a neighbor to worship.

16. Monday

Morning: Pray for our nation's leaders.
Evening: Read Mark 8.
Mercy: Visit a retirement or nursing home.

17. Tuesday

Morning: Pray for world leaders.
Evening: Read Genesis 9.
Mercy: Offer a word of encouragement to a family member.

18. Wednesday

Morning: Pray for teachers.
Evening: Read Mark 9.
Mercy: Offer a kind word to a store clerk.

19. Thursday

Morning: Pray for people in other countries.
Evening: Read Genesis 11.
Mercy: Offer an encouraging word to someone new to
        your country or community.

20. Friday

Morning: Pray for children and your church's children's ministry.
Evening: Read Mark 10.
Mercy: Do something nice for children in your congregation.

21. Saturday

Morning: Pray for those serving overseas.
Evening: Read Genesis 12.
Mercy: Write a note of encouragement to someone
        serving overseas.

22. Sunday
Morning: Worship.
Evening: Read Mark 11.
Mercy: Eat lunch with your family and be thankful.

23. Monday
Morning: Pray for those who are away from their homes.
Evening: Read Genesis 13.
Mercy: Learn and raise awareness about refugees.

24. Tuesday
Morning: Pray for those who feel rejected.
Evening: Read Mark 12.
Mercy: Do something kind for your next-door neighbor.

25. Wednesday
Morning: Pray for those who don't know God.
Evening: Read Genesis 14.
Mercy: Tell someone about God's love.

26. Thursday
Morning: Pray for a greater trust in God.
Evening: Read Mark 13.
Mercy: Make plans to volunteer at a homeless shelter.

27. Friday
Morning: Give thanks for God's promises.
Evening: Read Genesis 15.
Mercy: Make a covenant to help someone in need each
week.

28. Saturday
Morning: Pray about times when you have denied Jesus.
Evening: Read Mark 14.
Mercy: Visit a prison.

30-Day Means of Grace Challenge

29. Sunday

Morning: Worship.
Evening: Read Genesis 16.
Mercy: Write letters of encouragement to residents of a
        shelter for abused women.

30. Monday

Morning: Pray for those who are near death.
Evening: Read Mark 15.
Mercy: Visit a hospice center.

Churchwide Study and Intergenerational Activities

Six-week studies of Rueben P. Job's book *Three Simple Questions: Knowing the God of Love, Hope, and Purpose* are available for children, youth, and adults:

Adults

- *Three Simple Questions: Knowing the God of Love, Hope, and Purpose,* by Rueben P. Job
- DVD with Leader Guide

Youth

- *Three Simple Questions for Youth* (leader's guide)
- *Three Simple Questions for Youth* (student book)
- *Three Simple Questions: Knowing the God of Love, Hope, and Purpose*, by Rueben P. Job (optional)

Children

- *Three Simple Questions to Help Children Know God*

Intergenerational Activities

As you study *Three Simple Questions* with the adults, youth, and children of your congregation, you may want to plan for group involvement in intergenerational activities. Consider these possibilities:

- Plan a concluding celebration on a Sunday morning that will create a renewed commitment to asking and answering the basic questions of our faith. Recruit adults, youth, and children to offer testimonies about what they learned and practiced during their study.

- Add an intergenerational activity to each session. For example, the combined group might create a group banner for each of the three simple questions. The banners can then be displayed in the sanctuary during worship as a reminder of what the groups have learned.

- Make suggestions of songs or hymns that reflect the three simple questions and give to those who plan the worship services for the weeks following the study. Enlist someone to name the connections to the three simple questions when the songs are sung.

- Prepare a video or skits that illustrate the three simple questions. Involve actors from all age groups.

- Ask children, youth, and adults to work together to design the worship altar that reflects the meanings of the three simple questions in the lives of Christians.

About the Writer

Amy Valdez Barker is an ordained Deacon in the North Georgia Annual Conference of The United Methodist Church. She has been involved in youth ministry for the past fifteen years and is currently working on a Ph.D in Christian Education and Congregational Studies at Garrett-Evangelical Theological Seminary. Her passion is preparing and equipping students to live out their faith in meaningful and transformative ways. She loves God, loves her husband, Rich, and absolutely adores her two children, Ashtin and Tre.

Who Is God? | Who Am I? | Who Are We Together?

How we answer these three simple questions has a big impact on what we believe, how we live, and how we relate to other people.

In *Three Simple Questions for Youth*—based on Rueben P. Job's book *Three Simple Questions: Knowing the God of Love, Hope, and Purpose*—youth will spend six weeks discussing and wrestling with these basic but life-changing questions:

- **WHO IS GOD?** What do we know about God? What can we learn about God through the person of Jesus Christ and the ongoing presence of the Holy Spirit?

- **WHO AM I?** What does it mean for us to be God's beloved children? How do we reflect the light of Christ into the darkness we encounter?

- **WHO ARE WE TOGETHER?** What does it mean to be the church? How do we, as members of the church, practice our faith?

Three Simple Questions for Youth responds to these questions with a host of activities, challenges, and discussion questions. During these six sessions, youth will gain a better understanding of how to live as a child of God and a member of the body of Christ.

Also Available:

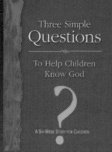

Three Simple Questions to Help Children

Three Simple Questions ISBN: 9781426741548

Three Simple Questions DVD with Leader Guide ISBN: 9781426742576

Three Simple Questions for Youth-Student ISBN: 9781426742606

Cokesbury®
Christian Bookstores

ISBN-13: 978-1-426-74261-3

90000

9 781426 742613